Hymn Primer

A Very Easy Book of Hymns
For Piano or Electronic Keyboard
By Wesley Schaum

Foreword

This book is designed to make familiar hymns as easy as possible. A student with just six to eight weeks study will be able to start enjoying this album.

The pieces are arranged in five-finger position with melody divided between the hands. A minimum of finger numbers is used. Large, widely spaced notes help make music reading easier. Rests have been purposely omitted so the student can focus on the notes.

Duet accompaniments offer many possibilities for recitals and Sunday school participation. The duets help provide rhythmic training and ensemble experience especially valuable to beginners. The person playing the accompaniment is free to add pedal according to his/her own taste.

The duets are recommended for use at home as well as at the lesson. However, the student should work alone at first until the notes and rhythm of the solo part are secure.

Index

Schaum Publications, Inc.

EXCLUSIVELY DISTRIBUTED BY

HAL•LEONARD®
CORPORATION
7777 W. BLUEMOUND RD. P.O. BOX 13819 MILWAUKEE, WI 53213

ISBN-13: 978-1-936098-63-7

09-30

Faith of Our Fathers

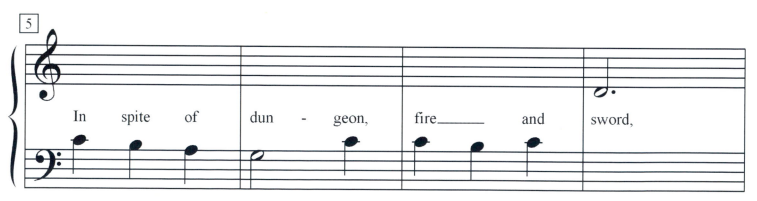

Duet Accompaniment (Stem up = R.H. Stem down = L.H.)

3

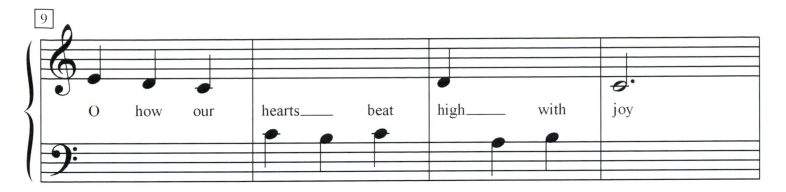

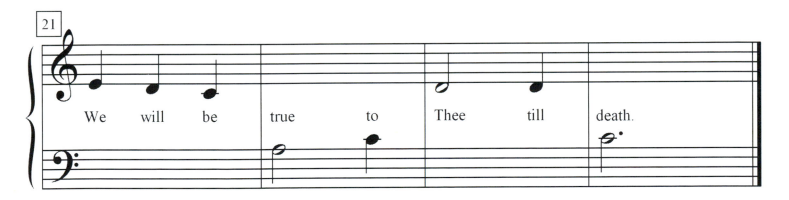

Duet Accompaniment (continued)

Jesus Loves Me This I Know

Fairest Lord Jesus

6

Tell Me the Stories of Jesus

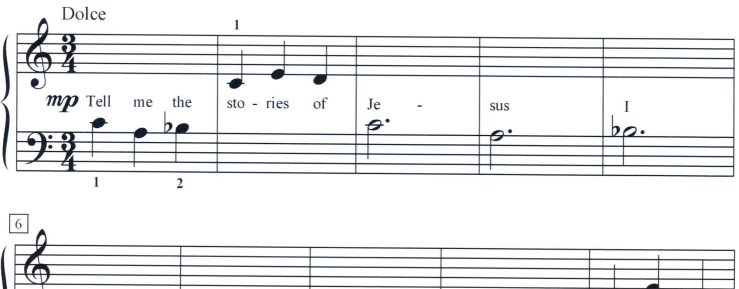

Dolce

mp Tell me the sto - ries of Je - sus I

love to hear; Things I would ask Him to

Duet Accompaniment

mp

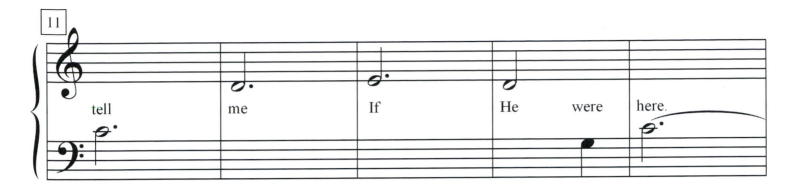

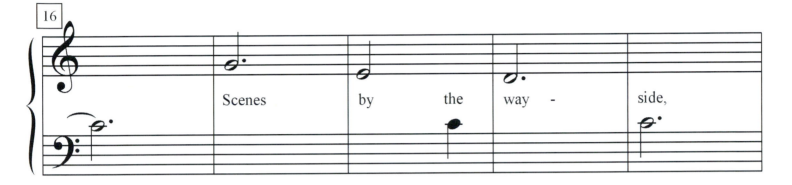

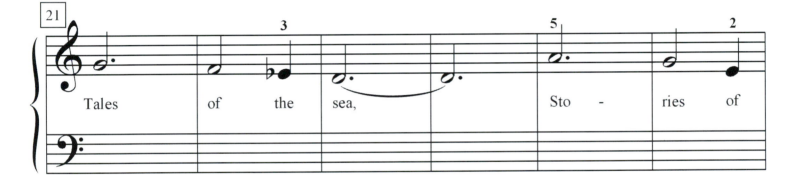

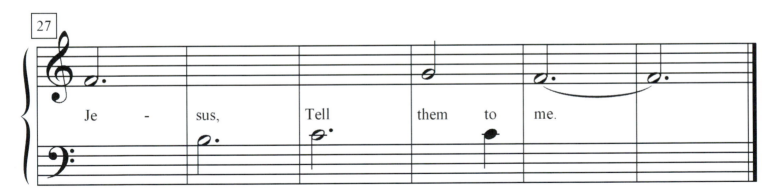

Duet Accompaniment (continued)

Now Thank We All Our God

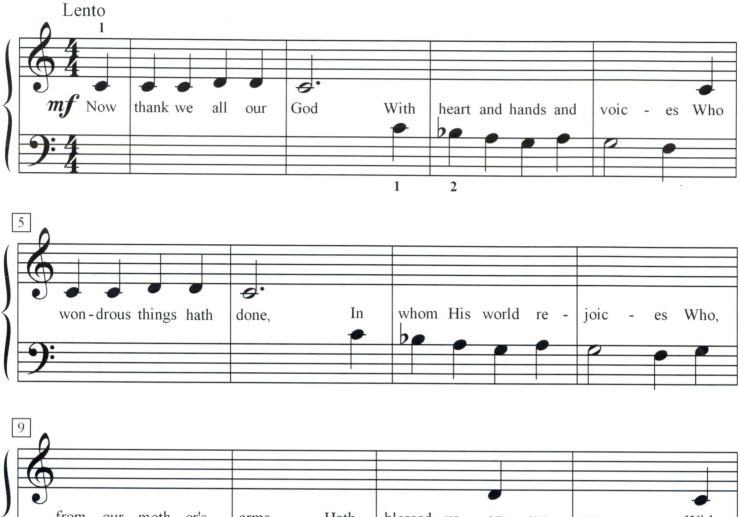

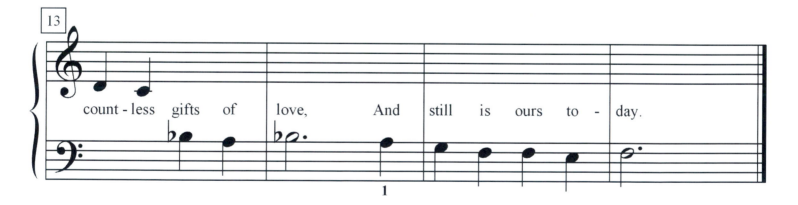

Duet Accompaniment

O Worship the King

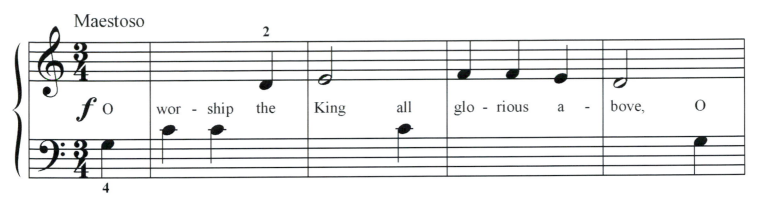

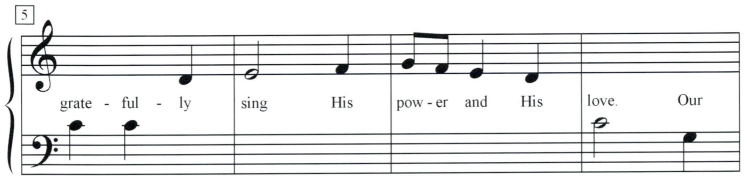

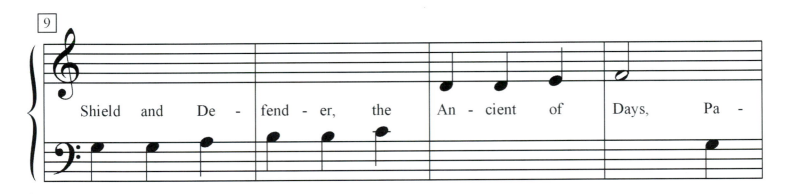

Duet Accompaniment

Praise to the Lord the Almighty

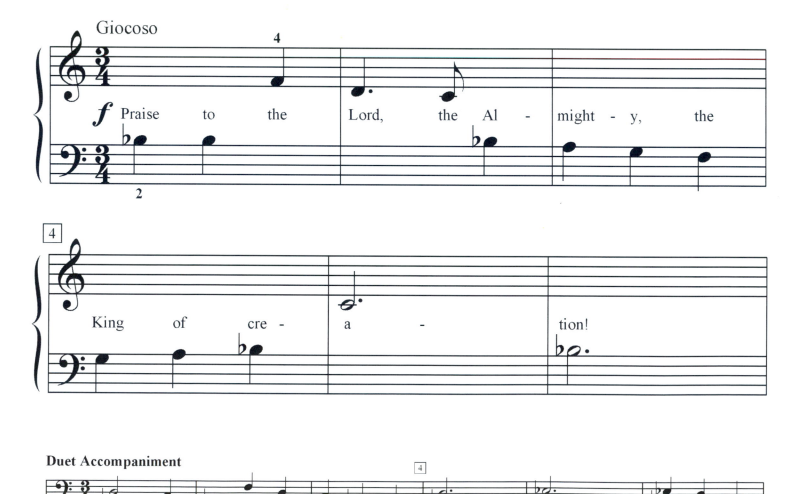

Giocoso

Praise to the Lord, the Al - might - y, the King of cre - a - tion!

Duet Accompaniment

Teacher's Note: If the pupil is in the early grades in school and has not yet had fractions, do not attempt to explain the dotted quarter note-eighth note rhythm. The rule to follow is this: *experience should precede explanation.* Teach the rhythm by rote. Delay the explanation until the situation arises at a later time when the student has acquired fraction readiness.

O my soul, praise Him for He is thy

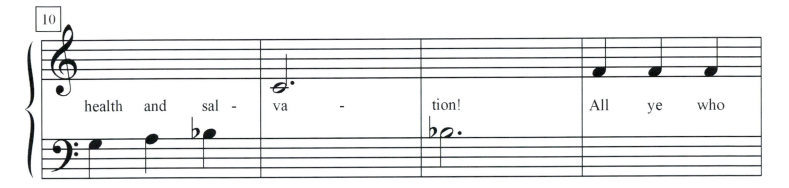

health and sal - va - tion! All ye who

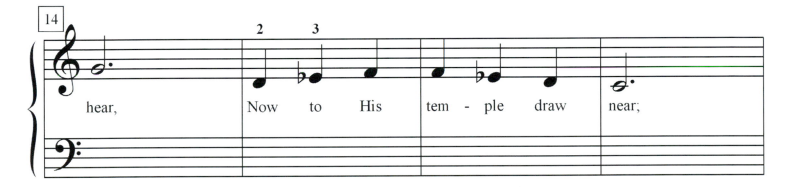

hear, Now to His tem - ple draw near;

Join me in glad ad - o - ra - tion.

Duet Accompaniment (continued)

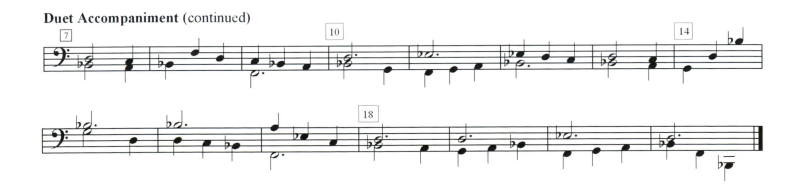

As With Gladness Men of Old

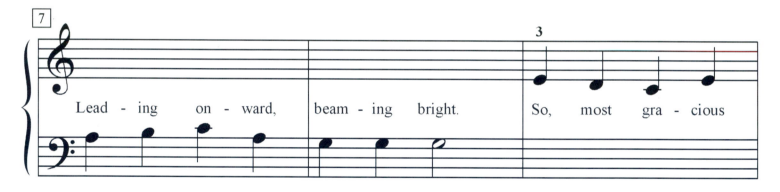

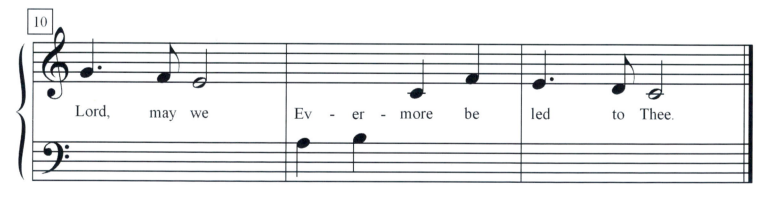

Duet Accompaniment

Holy, Holy, Holy!

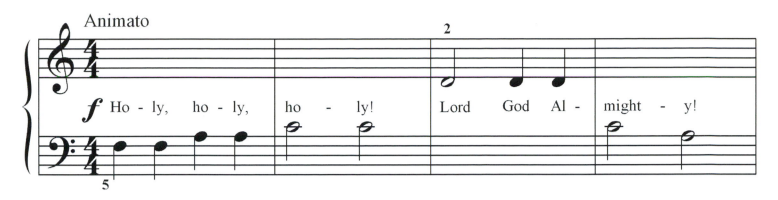

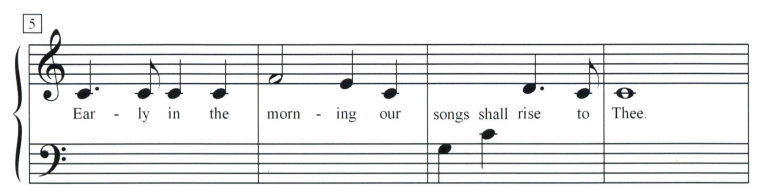

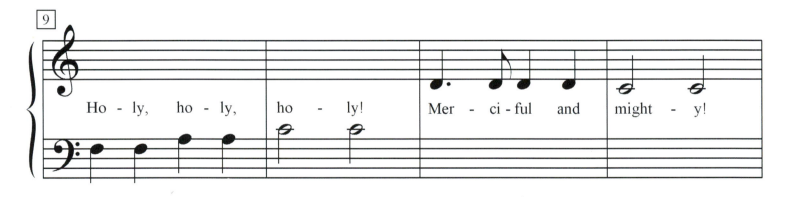

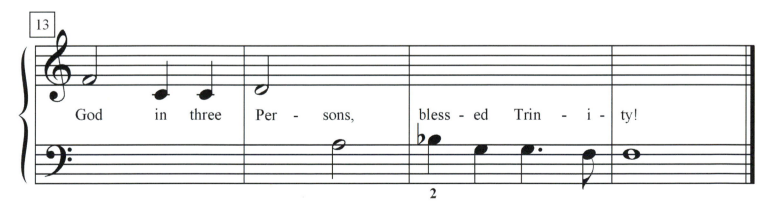

Duet Accompaniment

A Mighty Fortress Is Our God

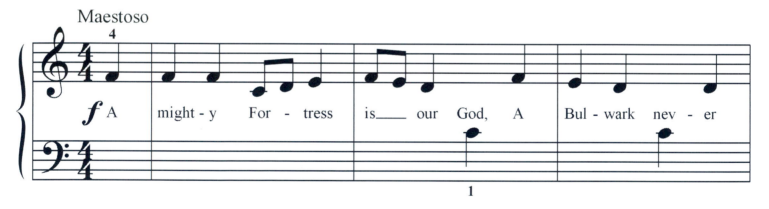

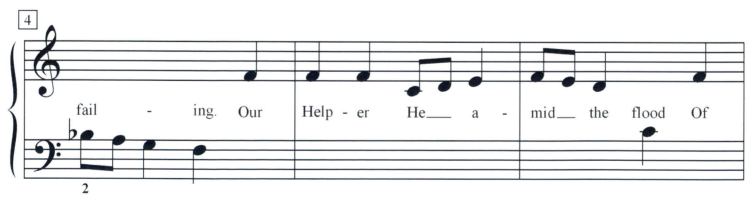

Duet Accompaniment

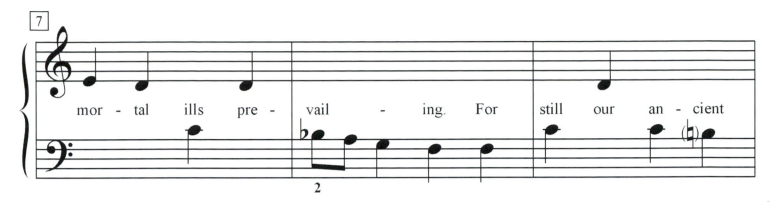

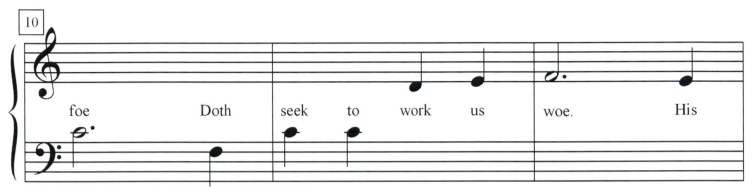

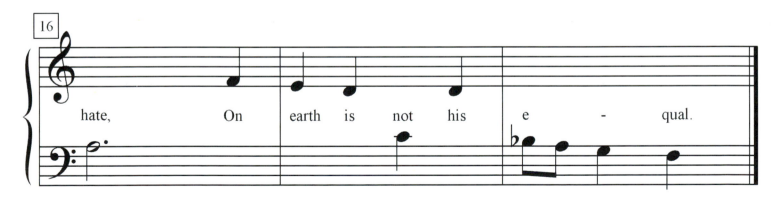

Duet Accompaniment (continued)

Take My Life and Let It Be

All Hail the Power of Jesus' Name

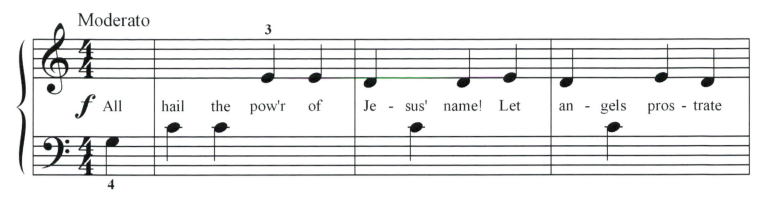

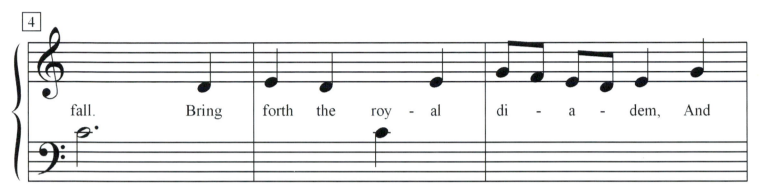

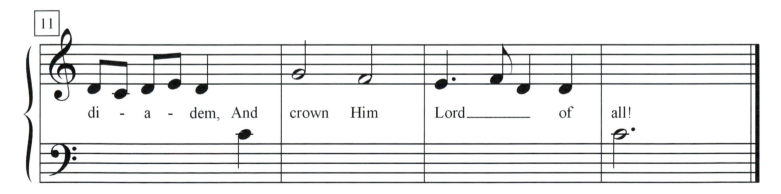

Duet Accompaniment

Glorious Things of Thee Are Spoken

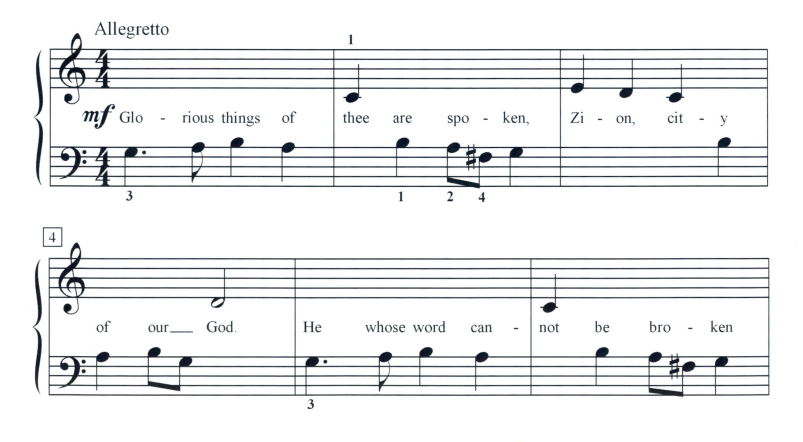

Allegretto

mf Glo - rious things of | thee are spo - ken, | Zi - on, cit - y

of our___ God. | He whose word can - | not be bro - ken

Duet Accompaniment

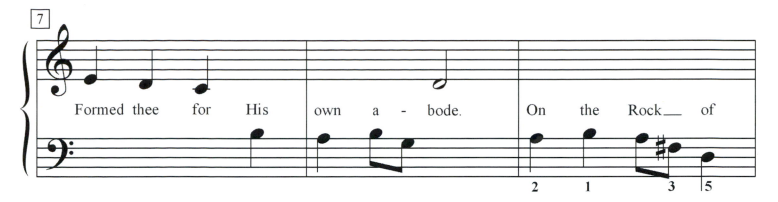

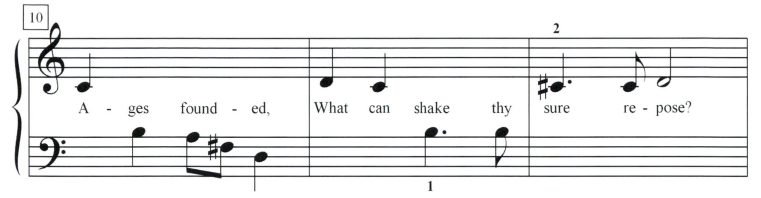

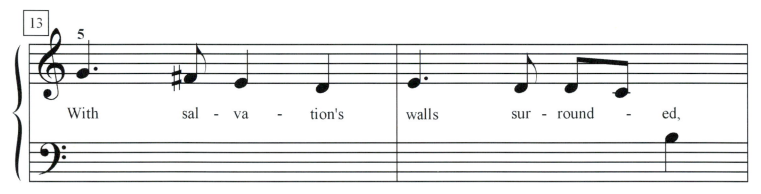

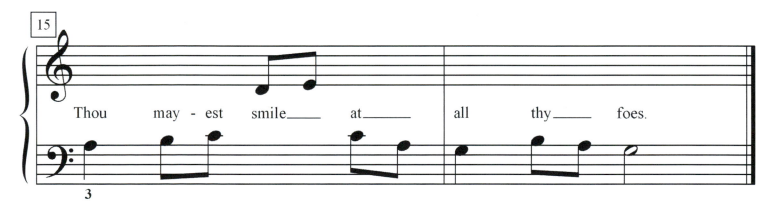

Duet Accompaniment (continued)

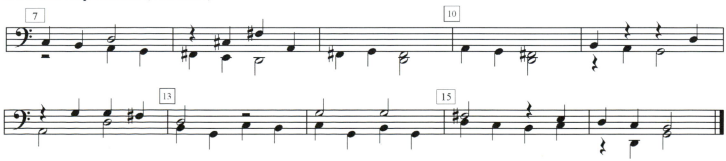

All Things Bright and Beautiful

Allegretto

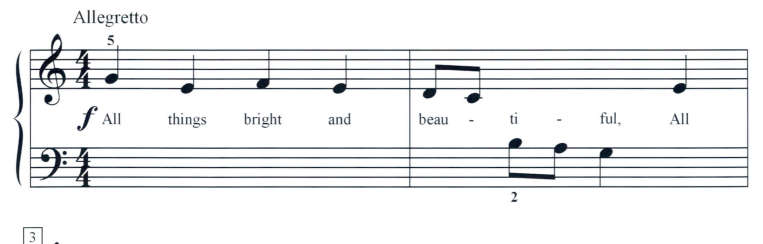

All things bright and beau - ti - ful, All

crea - tures great and___ small, All things wise and

Duet Accompaniment

won - der - ful, The Lord God made them____

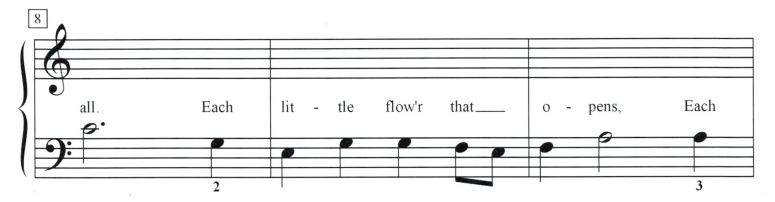

all. Each lit - tle flow'r that____ o - pens, Each

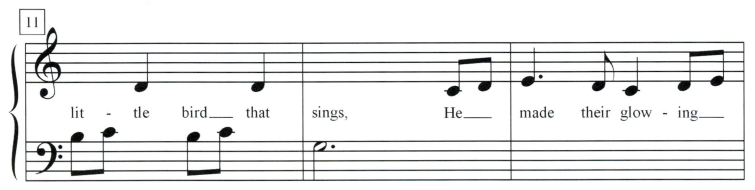

lit - tle bird____ that sings, He____ made their glow - ing____

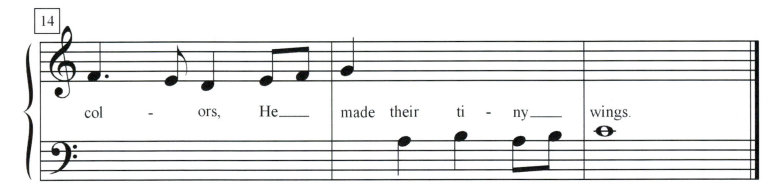

col - ors, He____ made their ti - ny____ wings.

Duet Accompaniment (continued)

This Is My Father's World

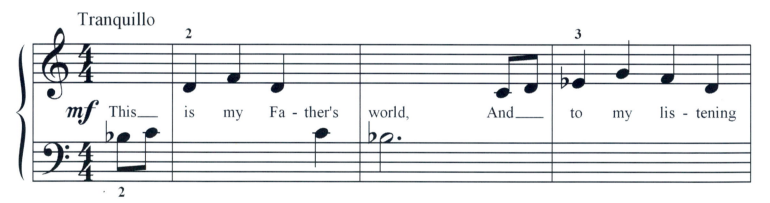

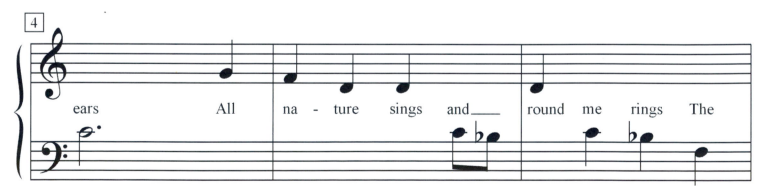

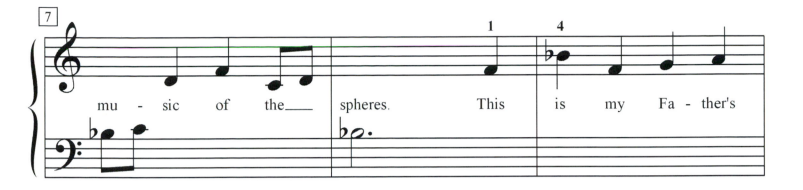

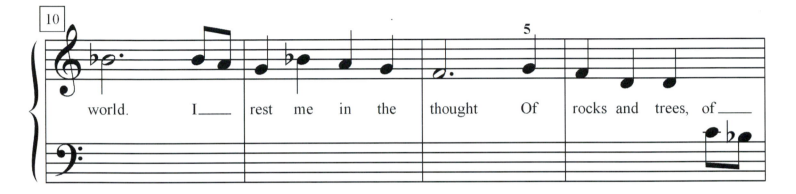

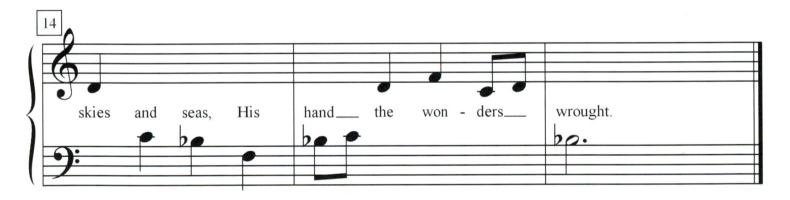

Duet Accompaniment (continued)

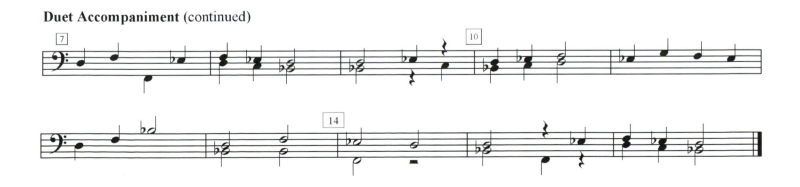